T0157559

JILLIAN'S

BY BEN MATICH

authorHOUSE®

AuthorHouse™
1663 Liberty Drive
Bloomington, IN 47403
www.authorhouse.com
Phone: 1-800-839-8640

First published by AuthorHouse 11/21/2011

ISBN: 978-1-4670-6153-7 (sc)

Printed in the United States of America

Any people depicted in stock imagery provided by Thinkstock are models,
and such images are being used for illustrative purposes only.
Certain stock imagery © Thinkstock.

This book is printed on acid-free paper.

*

<u>I DEDICATE THIS BOOK</u>
<u>TO MY RELIGION…</u>

TABLE OF CONTENTS

*

INTRODUCTION

Greetings, to all of my readers out there, and welcome back; to "Our" forum.

[This is my "<u>SIXTH</u>" book].

It is my hope, as We gather here, together today, that We will be able to push aside, all the superficial (build-ups)- blasted at each, and every one of Us, dosing vigorously, with (Falsisms); like "Honey" to the "Comb".

However, I am positively convinced though, that without Jill- in "My Life" before, I would not be, up to, many of the things; that I can do today.

She, is responsible, for My "Integral Successes" achieved- minimally, but not; to be diminished.

What I mean is, (Jill) may have done little things, but they meant a lot; to Me.

They, mattered more, than She- will ever know, and I, am grateful to Her; for this fact.

As they say, it's all about, the (Jill-Jill); Jillian…

By Ben Matich

JILL'S PONDER

(We) all watched, (We) all listened, even when-
it seemed, as if, it was; to no avail.

(We) tried, and tried, like (The Sailors)- who
just, wanted to go out, and sail, but could not, due
to, a "Major Ongoing"; and "Dangerous Storm".

Either way, we'd get up, our things- as if, to
accept, all of the sometimes, "Ill-Logic"; (He)
would project.

"Silly Gestures", "Upon Their Faces", were all
there- saying:

"[Hey; (Pull-Pull)]" !

At least, that is, until (He) exclaimed;

"No! No! No! No!"

I saw, (Her Face), as (Jill)- had lost, (Her Glow),
(I) too, became stunned, for (I) realized, just like

(She) did, at that moment, the place which (We), were at; wasn't always quite so fun...

By Ben Matich

*

<u>LTC</u>

Once, upon a time, (I) knew- this (Girl), a very, good friend, (She) was, to (Me), and (She) was; to (Jill).

I had, all types, of "Props"- for (Her), and "Respect", for (I), used to quietly, in awe, be watching, at all the times, that (She), would interject; abruptly and aloud.

(She), would blurt out, things occasionally- sometimes good, sometimes strange, either way, this was, keeping (Me), sort of, at a; "Shy's Distant Range".

(She'd) approach, (Me) first, always seeming- to open up, and (I), liked that mentality; about (Her).

[Once, (I) even got, the nerve- to get, "My Crude Chin"; up].

When the time, arrived though, (I) had- to think, to (Myself):

['No'].

Because, even when, (She) was already taken-(I) had, simply put; liked (Jill)…

By Ben Matich

*

<u>LTC : 2</u>

(I), am proud, to say- that (I), "Really Did", like hanging out, with (Jill); and (LTC).

I say, (Those Two), were not- exactly the type, who'd "Play Around", for (I), wouldn't recommend, the (Silly), going towards (Them); to be abound.

I learned, with (Them), probably- by "My Observations", (Who) is "Real"; and (Who) is "Fake".

Through, each "New Situation", that (They And I)- would be "Prepared"; to thereby "Intake".

Interactions were held, with (Brass And Tact), plus- (Jill's); "Great Smile"; what a fact!

Though hidden, (LTC) brought, it back out- of (Her), yet somewhat; "Unriled".

(I'll) add here:

['Word'; towards (Heather)].

But, remember this:

(These Girls), are not of, (The Dainty Women)- who would, have chosen to, correspond with (Me), by "Means"; of "A Feather".

Somewhere, along "The Line", (Yes)- (I Say-Yay), (Straight-And-Narrowly), through "The Truth", (I) realized, although it was, "Softly Acted Out", yet with "Care", what (The Three Of Us), had in common;

[They were hardcore]…

By Ben Matich

*

MOUNTAINS ARE MONOTONOUS

(Many), had suggested, to (Me)- that (I) should ask, but (I) did not want to, because it would, have been, more than "A Chore", for it, would have been; "A Great Big Task"!

I also, had known, "Deep Down"- but even more so, "Obviously", (Jill) was "Involved", and (I), didn't want, to be out of, "Good Character", so (Her) and (I), would be left, unfortunately; "Unresolved".

Unto (My Eyes), (I) would hold onto, "My Revere"- but not bring (It), ever, way too near, for (Jill), must not be "Burdened", and wasn't; with "My Discomforts".

Now (Jill), (I) can rejoice for, because- (She's) got, (Her Happiness), but (I) chose, not to adhere; with potential "Public Clapping-Ness".

I am glad, for (Jillian), "Woe-Be-To-Me"- as for (Her), (I) will smile, giving out, a "Sorrowful

Giggle"; which indeed, never had; contained "Glee"…

By Ben Matich

*

I SHOULD HAVE KNOWN, SHE WOULD NOT BE WITH ME

[There once, was "A Place", and it was- full of; "Arts And Supplies]".

(It) definitely, could be called, "Descriptive"- as (It) did be, of appeal, (Yes); to "Everybody's Surprise".

"Other Senses", would arise too, for it was- pretty much, that kind of "Environment", and (I), liked "The Weirdness", that was, going on "There"; oddly enough.

I was busy, washing my hands, and yes- it was most assuredly; "A Numerous Amount"; of times.

I usually do, keep "My Hands", "Very Clean"- to (My Demise) though, "The Host", of (This Area), was proportionately; a "Tad Bit" mean.

I was angry, but then, (Some Girl)- pops up, to (Me), and says, to relax, and forget, about whatever it was, that (I) had been; so "Fixated" on.

I couldn't believe; (Her Nerve)! (Keeping In Mind), that (I), did not- even "Know", (This Person), and (She) was more, than just; "A Little Bold-Faced"!

"Admiration", then kicked in, (I) was going- to go, for "The Gold", so to speak, (Me And My Question), but (Someone), had already beaten (Me); to it.

Much to, "My Misfortune", (They)- were inquiring, about (Patricia's), "Soon-To-Be"; "Newly Betrothed" plans.

(Ladies And Gentlemen), please understand, how "Shocked"- and "Dismayed", (I) was; at that moment.

[Ok]?

It was 100% true! The (Girl), was "Totally", and "Absolutely"; "Engaged"...

By Ben Matich

*

BEING AWAY FROM IT ALL

It had been, quite awhile,well-at least (A Year), and (I'd) thought; about things.

But; 'Nay'!

['Word', to being against, a (Fresh) and a ; "New-Bound Cheer"]!

Though (I) was, called out properly, (I) will leave things- (Well Enough Alone), such as, past dealings; with (Chad).

Even when, (We) "Suspect, (We) should not-wander around, in (Life), looking all over, the place for, more and more; "Little Lies".

[You may end, up uncovering, some; "Big Ones" instead].

For, "The Breakup", along with "The Breakings"- were too much, to handle, alongside the accompaniment, of (Elizabeth's), "Dreaded Cries", (Forever) held, to only be heard; by (I).

["Their Consistency", seemed to revolve, about how (I); did not "Care"].

After, (That Green Glass Bottle), was thrown-over "My Head", (I) do remember later on, after things had calmed, quite down, (I) recall how (I), went back "Outside", in "The Yard", where (It); had been left.

[I picked, (It) up, and looked; at (It)].

I guess, (I) could have, figured this out- all on "My Own", but wait; yes wait.

I can not, anymore talk, for (I)- keep forgetting, that now, (I) am only, (The Mouse), for (I) am, (Truly) no longer; (The Hawk)...

By Ben Matich

*

THE NINGA B KNEW

The following, was "A Nightmare", which (I) had- a while ago, but (It) had indeed, "Posed Itself", as "Very Real"; unto (Me).

[For, (I) believe, that this was, some kind of, "Burglary", occurring on; "Dream's Time".

In (The Night), "My Yellowed Eyes", had spotted- familiar, "Pale Green Skin", which "Motioned", towards "Ghastly White", as (The Ninga), was "Hoppen"; and "Hippen".

Up (The Chimney), "Suit" and all, just like (Santa)- only dressed, in "Black", seemingly to (Me), to be giving out, "Vibes", of ; "ENTHRALL"!

[I had yelled; to 'Halt']!

However, "This Pursued Figure", simply kept- skipping from, (One House Top), to another, "Upwalled" and "Uninterested", in what (I), had just said; to (Them).

I then, brought out, "My Piece"- and even though, (I) did receive, the "Feeling", that (I) should "Cease", (I) was "Ready"; and "Stead Fast".

At that, "Exact Moment", (I) began to "Stammer"- at the sight, of "A New Found Problem", which was, safe to say; "Unexpected".

As (One), of (The Boys), took off (Her Mask)- (We All) were looking, at what was "Printed",on (Her Clothing):

"[BETHABE", for (Elizabeth); this was]...

By Ben Matich

*

<u>WHERE IS THY, JILL ?</u>

"Christmas Carols", are so very cool, to be (Singing)- and (Listening) to, because of, "The Harmonious Aspects", which (They) indeed, do "Deliver"; and "Provide".

I generally,will find (Myself), kind of- making up, "My Own Words", to "The Selected Rhythms", because (I) can't ever, seem to "Memorize", what gets presented, unto (Me); in "The First Place".

(Jill) had believed, (One) should "Over-Surmount", (Their Fears), of being "Exposed", to "The Inclusiveness"; of "A Public Place".

I have to, wonder though, if (She) understood, "How Difficult", for (Me), to keep up, with (Her), in "That Regard", thus would actually be; however.

It can be said, that (Jill), might have "Grasped It"- (She) also; might not have.

43

[I don't know, which one, it ended up; as though].

I am, "Trained Better", than to tell (LTC)- on (You), (Jillian); yikes! But, (I) also, should say this:

'Oh no'! 'Never mind, for (I) am seeing, all of a sudden- (My Existence), flashing before; (My Very Eyes)!

[(My), "Coca Cola's", are getting; "Stale"]`!!!

By Ben Matich

*

<u>CONCLUSION</u>

Well, that's it. We are at the end, of the road; again. We've reached (Our) stop, and it is now time, to get off, the (B Bus); for right now.

Buy more books, and there will be more rides; right? The price of admission, is supporting my material, and I'll be writing; more of it.

Don't, and I won't. That's how it goes; these days.

(Hee-Hee-Hee)!

Until, the next time, we are out, of (B's Creed), so do; take care…

By Ben Matich

*

<u>BONUS</u>

<u>~FAVORITE QUOTES, THIS AUTHOR BELIEVES, WHOLE- HEARTEDLY IN, AND TRIES TO LIVE BY, EACH DAY</u>:

-) I only pick one letter, out of the Alphabet; to really get into. Can I help that the letter "I", means the most to me?

-) I ask you all, who is the "Krim Da La Krim"?

P.s.) (Tinaaaa), play fair; now...

-) I am a Martian, and please don't ask me why...

-) Don't ask me about the "Fundamentals"; because I don't know.

-) (Sing-Songingly), I say: I don't know, I don't care, I don't know; and I don't care...

-) Word to the "Clickages".

*(<u>ANNNDDD</u>),, <u>(LAST BUT NOT LEASSSSTTT</u> !

*) Nobody, cracks Me up; like "I" can...

(The End).

*

OTHER BOOKS BY THIS AUTHOR

~Heavenly Struck
~Heavenly Struck (Vol.2)
~Golden Treacherys
~The Pinnacle Of My Life
~B's No Good
.

`These books are available to buy at "Author House". Call (1-888-519-5121).`

`These books, can also be bought; at "Amazon. Com".

"Plus, you can also, try to buy them; at (Abe Books.Com)".

~Oh yeah, and don't forget, if you can not find my books, in your local bookstores, ask for them, to see if they can be ordered~...

Thanks.